CRAFTING YOUR PITCH

CRAFTING YOUR PITCH

A Storytelling Framework

Joanne Tombrakos

Crafting Your Pitch, a Storytelling Framework
Joanne Tombrakos

Copyright © 2023
Joanne Tombrakos
Ansonia Station
PO Box 230398
New York, NY 10023

Book design: Glen Edelstein

For information on obtaining permissions for reprints and excerpts, contact the publisher at the above address.

Paperback: 978-0-9840076-7-7
eBook: 978-0-9840076-8-4

Printed and bound in the United States of America

For my father who taught me the power of good storytelling and to my mother for always reminding me to be my best.

CONTENTS

PROLOGUE

I grew up in a family of storytellers. My father could spin a yarn and engage his audience better than anyone I have ever seen. His stories of growing up in Brooklyn watching the Dodgers play at Ebbets Field and "slinging hot dogs" at Coney Island made you feel you were there right alongside him. He elaborated on the lore that our ancestors fled from Crete in a boat one night to escape the Turks during the Ottoman Empire. His explanation of how the family wound up in the Peloponnese area of Greece was so convincing that I believe there is truth to it. He could weave a tale on the spot about whatever happened on his way home from work. The stories came out of him so easily that they pulled you in, making you want to hear more.

My father knew how to use story to engage.

He stood six foot one inches tall, with a barrel chest, a hearty laugh, and an energy that made everyone turn when he walked through the door. He knew how to read a room and play to his audience. He loved to talk, but he also loved to listen and observe. While his ultimate goal was to persuade someone to smile, he provoked curiosity and had a way of getting you to think and ask him to show you why things were a certain way or how they worked. Whoever was sitting in front of him felt as if they were the most important person in the world.

He used story to do that.

My father understood that to capture his audience's full attention, he had to bring them into the story. While authenticity might be an overused word today, my father was the real deal. He never pretended to be anyone but himself. His enthusiasm was contagious. There was no question he relished every minute of his time with you. He enjoyed the story he was telling so much it was hard for whomever was listening not to enjoy it as well.

I had no idea that these traits that I observed as a young girl growing up in Glen Oaks Village, on the outskirts of Queens in New York City, would translate into learned skills that I would use both personally and professionally throughout my life.

Unlike my Dad, I was painfully shy growing up. As a young girl, I kept most of my thoughts to myself with the exception of my family and closest friends. In elementary school, my teachers told my mother I was a leader. I rejected that notion and chose to speak only when spoken to in any environment that made me uneasy, which was just about everywhere outside of my own home. I was that insecure. The idea of being the storyteller and not the audience could literally make me break out in hives.

For a long time, I continued to observe. It was not until I embarked on a career in media advertising sales that things changed. If I wanted to succeed and earn a living, I had to find a way to sell that was both effective and comfortable for me.

Success did not come easily to me. I needed to learn what would lead to a sale and gain the confidence to tell an effective story. It took time for me to fully integrate those elements. I needed to understand myself, my product, and my client. After years of therapy and a preoccupation with self-improvement, it became easier for me to build out a convincing pitch. I came to realize that a good pitch involves telling a good story—one that has purpose, that engages an audience, keeps them there, and persuades them you are worth listening to. It was what I had observed in my father growing up.

My father taught me how to tell a story with a clear beginning, middle, and end. He never wrote those elements down on a piece of paper and explained what a story arc was, but I understand now that is what I was observing in his natural talents. He never just told a story; he "sold" his story to an audience he had succeeded in captivating.

I used his storytelling techniques to sell advertising opportunities to countless marketing executives and media buyers in every industry sector for 25 years. I represented radio and television stations and worked at media companies that included the Beasley Broadcast Group, CBS Radio, TimeWarner Cable, and NY1 News. I also served as an independent marketing consultant and sold my own services. The one commonality, throughout all that work, was that I sold using story.

This technique also became an important tool when I started teaching marketing to graduate students at New York University (NYU). I looked at each lecture as a pitch. What did I want my students to walk away with at the end of each two-and-a-half-hour session? How could I keep them engaged? What was the story arc for each week? How did all that roll up into a larger story at the end of the semester, fulfilling course objectives?

The process I developed involved four modalities, all integrated together: pitching, storytelling, presenting, and teaching. They are part art and part science that's supported by research, data, and insights. The commonality between all four modalities is the story arc. At the start of the curve, a problem is presented, followed by a way to solve that problem, and finally a resolution.

There is a tendency in the business world to think of pitching as something that is exclusive to sales teams. That is far from the truth. Everyone in an organization is pitching something, whether it is the latest research in your industry, the annual budget, or a new idea on how the company can run more effectively. I believe that learning how to pitch is the single most critical way to achieve success—whether you are selling a product, a service, an idea, or yourself.

What I have seen along the way both in my corporate life, and now in my teaching, is that most people don't know how to do this. No one really teaches the art of the pitch, and how to craft a pitch. We throw out a lot of data and tactics. We try and dazzle our audience with technology and fancy power point slide presentations that bore the audience we want to engage. We complicate things that need to be simplified. We focus so much on the outcome that we forget the process.

We reject the word pitch because it implies something too salesy and distasteful. We think storytelling is just telling a story, without considering its true purpose. This has become even more challenging in a world in which pitches are conducted virtually and in-person.

The need for proper pitching skills was driven home to me when I began teaching a course called the Real-World Strategic Partnership in 2018 at the NYU School of Professional Studies. During the course, students must solve a brief given to them by an actual company. Over a 14-week semester students work in teams to come up with an idea that solves the problem. They pitch it to the client, who then decides which team came up with most actionable solution. The executives who take part in the program have represented brands like Nike, ESPN, and Anheuser Busch. The classes I teach have partnered with Porsche NA, Samsung, jetBlue, and Ernst & Young.

Coming up with an idea is challenging. Solutions to problems need to be researched and thought out. Insights from the research give us the reasons that justify why our idea is so great. However, the most arduous part is figuring out how to craft and ultimately pitch that idea in a story that engages and sells.

I have watched my students struggle with the process. They want a template that prompts them to fill in the blanks. And presto! They have a pitch. However, templates can stifle creativity. A good pitch is a creative endeavor that conveys an idea. While I'm not a fan of templates, I do believe in frameworks, or outlines. So I initially helped my students by creating a Pitch Checklist that helped them develop a pitch framework. It was a tool to better understand the flow and arc of crafting a good pitch. My goal was to take some of the mystery out of it.

Some great novelists choose not to use outlines as part of their storytelling process. They work organically, letting the story develop as they write. But that doesn't work for pitches. When you craft a pitch, you are writing a story with a definitive purpose. You know exactly where it will end. It's the middle that's fuzzy. You need to begin with a framework to create your story arc, and eventually you'll eliminate that fuzziness.

My students have told me my checklist has helped them enormously. In fact, one student told me it was "pure gold." It was because of that encouragement that I decided to build on the checklist and create a Storytelling Framework.

Whether you are a student, a marketer, or anyone with a good idea that you want to sell, this book is for you. In essence, it's the secret sauce that uses elements of story to create a persuasive, compelling pitch that sells.

WHO THIS BOOK IS FOR

At the time I sat down to write this book, I wanted to help my students learn how to create better marketing pitches. And at the same time, I wanted to think through all the elements that go into effective pitches so I could better teach them. However, the more I wrote the more I realized that its significance goes beyond that. Crafting more engaging pitches and purposeful stories is something we all need to improve if we want to effect change.

To get our messages across in a deafeningly noisy world, we need to get our heads out of our phones and take the necessary time to think through the best ways to influence the people who could "buy" whatever we're trying to sell. We need to go beyond the pitch and understand the why. We need to listen, and we need to think—two soft skills that are often overlooked in our technologically driven world. Both are increasingly important as we try to balance out the noise and make sense out of the confusion. We have to differentiate ourselves from AI.

While this book is written from the perspective of pitching a marketing idea, its usefulness extends well beyond that. The story arc framework that I describe can help guide you through a formal presentation, take an entrepreneurial idea to market, or build momentum among key decisionmakers or staff members for change within an organization. The arc itself could also be used for more informal pitches, right down to the one that presents you as a candidate for a job.

Not all pitches involve power point presentations in a fancy board room or flat-screen technology. Some happen without WIFI connections. They can take place on an airplane, sitting at a bar—and yes, occasionally in an elevator if the person you are pitching manages to look up from their phone. There's one universal aspect to all great pitches, no matter how informal or formal they may be: you have put time and effort into thinking through your story. It has to become muscle memory.

The key to effective pitching is always agility, being able to think and act in the moment. You can rely on a prepared script and what the next slide says. That does not mean skimping on research, preparation, and practice. They are all critical. But in addition to that, you have to take the time to craft a pitch, and you have to start with a good story arc. That is what this book will show you how to do.

HOW TO USE THIS BOOK

There are two different ways you can use this book: for formal or informal pitches.

Formal pitches occur when you are lucky enough to speak with an intended audience in-person, and agile enough to switch to Zoom at the last minute and be just as effective. They could focus on a marketing campaign, a new product line, a solution to a business problem, or a plan for taking a new business idea to market. After reading this book, you'll be able to create a presentation that will both engage your audience and sell your idea while keeping within a 20-minute block of time. Twenty minutes is long enough to present a convincing pitch and short enough for an audience to grasp what your idea is.

Informal pitches occur when you don't have the ability to give a 20-minute pitch. Sometimes you will be presented with an opportunity to pitch your idea, your business, or yourself on the spur of the moment. And it may come when you least expect it.

By taking the time to craft that pitch in advance, as you would a formal pitch, you have a much greater chance of seizing that moment and coming across as authentic and human. You've taken the time to think things through. You know what you bring to the table and how you can help someone or their business. You practice it and internalize it so that it never sounds pitchy or salesy. It just sounds like you and your truth.

Keep in mind that this is a framework, not a template. There are no quick fixes when it comes to a good pitch. While you might be able to tailor or customize an existing pitch in the moment, there is no such thing as crafting a great pitch in under an hour, though many on the internet will try and sell that concept to you. A good pitch is part art and part science. It is a creative endeavor, and like all things creative, a process.

"Winning isn't everything but wanting to win is."

—Vince Lombardi

PART 1
Before You Start

Setting the stage is essential for any good story. When done well, it draws us in and holds our attention and keeps us wanting to know more. The same is true for any good pitch.

Before we dive into the framework that will help you develop a story arc and craft your pitch, there are some things that you need to consider.

My Dirty Little Secret

Here's a dirty little secret about me: I never really sold anyone anything. That is the truth.

Yet I spent 25 years working in one of the most cutthroat businesses: selling radio and then television advertising. I represented The Beasley Broadcast Group, CBS, and Time Warner. And I was very successful doing so.

So how did I do that without *selling?* I listened. I asked questions. *A lot of questions.*

I empathized with clients. I knew my stuff. *Inside and out.* What I didn't know, I made sure to learn. I knew my competition.

I looked for points of connection—not just between the client and their needs but between me and my client. I presented myself as someone there to help their business. I cared. I followed up. I said what I would do, then did it.

I connected a lot of dots. I looked for the opportunities. I was curious. I curated relevant information that would help my cause before curation was trendy and long before it was easy to send an email with a link to an article.

I built my personal brand, becoming someone my clients could trust to really help their business. Although in those days we didn't call it personal branding; we called it building a reputation that preceded you wherever you went.

Most importantly I learned how to tell a story that convinced potential buyers that what I had to offer was going to help them achieve their goals. In other words, I explained how my radio or TV station had an idea that would help them grow their business.

I never *sold* anyone anything, but I did close an awful lot of deals and make a lot of money. My approach was to present myself as someone who wanted to help their business, and I used story to explain how I could do that. Some people like to call this the "new" way of selling, but in fact the very best salespeople have been doing this all along.

Everything Is a Pitch
Everything

That truth might make you feel uncomfortable. It might have you squirming in your seat with a knot of anxiety in the pit of your stomach. It might have you wondering why you ever picked up this book. Pitching may not be the vision you have for your career path. However, everybody pitches, and if success is what you are after, you need to get good at this. So, I will say it again.

Everything is a pitch.

We all do it, all the time, not just people who are paid to generate revenue.

A job interview is a pitch. *You are pitching why you are the best qualified candidate for the job.*

A first date is a pitch. *You are pitching yourself as a great potential partner.*

A blog is a pitch. *You are pitching a viewpoint, and you want to convince others to agree, or at least to understand.*

Answering a question that's posed in a class assignment is a pitch. *You are pitching your answer with reasoning behind it.*

Trying to get your kid to eat broccoli when they hate it is a pitch.

A presentation is a pitch. *Every time you are trying to convince someone of something you are delivering a pitch.*

This book is a pitch. *Its intention is to give you more than a framework* to craft a great pitch. Its purpose is also to show you why this solution is a good one and why learning to present well is an essential business skill. Let's see how well I do.

PRO TIP: "The one thing people should always remember when pitching is that people remember stories much more than a list of facts."

—Bahriye Goran-Gulek, Clinical Associate Professor, Marketing, NYU,
Former Consumer Packaged Goods Marketing
and Branding Agency Executive

Selling Without "Selling"

If pitching means selling, then we need to reframe the word. "Sell" may be a four-letter word, but it is not one of the seven dirty words that you can never say on television, which the comedian George Carlin listed in his legendary monologue in 1972. Yet, that is how so many people approach the idea of selling, as if it is a dirty word.

Smart, creative entrepreneurs and corporate executives alike tend to disparage the word. I've heard them react to it by saying:

"Selling is so icky."

"Oooh, I can't sell."

"I'm not a salesperson."

"Let someone else do the selling."

"There are a lot of things I'm good at—but selling is not one of them."

"I could never do *that!*"

"Just hearing the word makes me break out in hives."

"I hate salespeople."

"No one wants to be sold to anymore."

That last response is true. No one wants to be sold to anymore—especially Millennials and Gen Z. And yet we live in a very noisy 24/7, interconnected world in which everyone has a voice and a platform where they can be heard and where the skinny on who you really are or what your business is about is nothing more than a Google search away. The truth is we are all selling all the time—even if we don't want to admit it.

The key to selling is to craft an effective pitch that doesn't feel pitchy. There are some individuals that can wing it wherever they may be, but in a world obsessed with data most of us need to present more than a slick song and dance that may or may not have any substance behind it. The majority of us need a pitch backed by insights learned from data. The bonus is that when we have data to support our reasoning (especially those of us who detest the idea of selling) we build confidence in our idea, our product, or service. And what we are actually doing is telling a story whose purpose is to persuade and convince.

In order to deliver an effective pitch that we feel comfortable selling, we have to craft it. This requires thought, research, and creativity. This will allow us to position our pitch as a solution to a problem, not just a way for us to make a quick buck. And whomever you're speaking with won't feel like they're being pitched to.

Instead, they will feel like you've:
- Invited them in.
- Enrolled them in your idea.
- Educated.
- Influenced.
- Captivated.
- Inspired.
- Engaged.
- Persuaded.
- Enticed.
- Seduced.
- Solved one (or more) of their problems.
- Opened their eyes to a problem they didn't know they had.
- Told them a really good story—with a purpose.

In other words, you've sold them, and yet they never fell sold to, and you never felt "salesy."

To pitch is to sell. If you are like most people and you hate those words, I suggest that it's time to get it over it.

TRY THIS: Open your LinkedIn messages. If your inbox is like mine, it is overflowing with unsolicited pitches. Try to find one that is engaging and relevant enough that it will make you want to respond. (*Hint: It won't be easy!*)

A Pitch Is an Argument

If you look up "argument" in the dictionary, you'll find several definitions. The one we tend to think of most frequently is what Merriam-Webster describes as "an angry quarrel or disagreement." It's what you can witness on any given day on social networks in the form of senseless banter that often goes nowhere and without resolution.

A second definition offered by *Merriam-Webster* is "a coherent series of reasons, statements, or facts intended to support or establish a point of view." That is the kind of argument you want to make when writing a pitch.

A pitch is an argument. It raises a question that needs to be answered or a problem that needs to be solved. It offers an answer or a solution to the problem raised. The goal is to convince and persuade someone that your solution is valid. Supportive data helps to validate each reason. And the points you make are driven home by the rule of three (which I'll get into shortly). An effective pitch proves that your answer to the raised question is valid and deserves consideration. And hopefully, it will change minds.

Bear in mind that a good pitch recognizes that there is always more than one solution to a problem. Include the three most important reasons your idea solves a certain challenge. Acknowledge the risks that a given solution may pose and anticipate those risks before the people you are pitching have a chance to raise an objection. You've answered it in advance.

For each solution (or point) that you present, provide three pieces of data that support your reasoning. A good argument cites data sources. It ends with a conclusion that ties back to the original argument posed and shows a crystal-clear understanding of the position that you've taken. When that's accomplished, the person you're pitching is apt to pause and think.

TRY THIS: Think of something you want to convince somebody to do. It can be an actual pitch you are working on or something as simple as choosing the movie you want to stream with your family on Netflix tonight.

List three reasons your idea is the best one. Then come up with three reasons for the other side of the argument.

Remember: if you don't understand and appreciate the opposing viewpoint, you will never convince anyone of your argument.

The Rule of Three

You may have noticed that I am a bit obsessed with the number three. It probably started when I was a child, raised in the Greek Orthodox faith. Everything seemed to be repeated in multiples of three, starting with the sign of the cross. I never thought of it in a business sense until I started selling ads on WXTU, a country music radio station in Philadelphia. While there, I was taught that when presenting a radio campaign proposal to a client, I should always have three levels of choice. One should be exactly within the budget that was given. One should be a little less expensive and a third should be over budget.

Three options was the perfect amount of choice to offer, I was told at the time. Anything more would confuse my potential buyer. Just one would make it too easy to say yes or no to my offer. Three allowed me to end my pitch by asking which choice they liked best. This tactic is what's known as "assuming the close."

At the time I had no idea that the power of three also pertains to the three-act structure in storytelling. And I wasn't aware that the rule of three is commonly used in communication to make messages resonate. The concept dates back to Aristotle, who identified three types of persuasion in his treatise, *Rhetoric*. They include logos (logic), pathos (emotion), and ethos (credibility). He also noted that a good argument consisted of three parts.

That logic made sense to me.

It makes even more sense when you consider the overwhelming number of choices we are presented with each day. If you're not sure what I mean just walk into CVS and try to buy a tube of toothpaste. The easy part is knowing what brand you prefer, but once you have gotten that far there are more choices to consider. Let's say your brand of preference is Colgate. The next choice is which product line, Colgate Total, Optic White, Enamel Health, Max-Fresh, Sensitive, or Activate Charcoal. If you settle on Optic White, then you must further choose between Optic Pro, White Renewal, Advanced Whitening, and Stain Fighting. It shouldn't be so hard to determine the difference—much less decide between tubes of toothpaste—but it is.

Because toothpaste is something we need, we'll make a choice, even if it is confusing and we are pressed to think too much before coming to a decision. We pull one option off the shelf that we hope is the best choice, even if we are not fully convinced.

That doesn't happen when pitching ideas. We will never gain the attention of our audience (much less hold it) if we give too many choices. Instead, we need to zero in on the most important insights that we have uncovered and what is key to building our case.

We live in an extremely noisy world with a thousand messages beamed to us daily through the magic of technology. It's too easy to get distracted. When pitching, we want to break through the noise and keep it simple. Three is a manageable number.

Bear in mind that as our attention spans continue to shrink, we look for options that catch our attention and engage us. That's why we can lose an entire weekend to Netflix, a bag of popcorn and our couch.

When outlining your argument, you want to first grab the attention of your intended audience. Then focus on the three most important reasons why your idea is a good one. Each reason should be supported by three insights you garnered from the data you uncovered in your research. You will see how this works when we move to Part Two of this book and begin crafting our pitch.

PRO TIP: "When pitching put yourself in the shoes, seats and minds of your audience. Start with their why, not your why."

—Linda Descano, Executive Vice President, of the Media Agency Red Havas

The Story Arc

I started calling myself a storyteller long before it became trendy. When I left my corporate life in 2008, I did a number of things. In addition to writing, I was consulting, which involved selling my services. It was during this period that I first began educating others, leading workshops. That can be quite challenging, in a world of short attention spans. I needed to figure out how to convey information in as few words as possible, without overcomplicating things. Teaching involved engaging other people in ways that provoked conversation. That's when I realized that I was a storyteller.

It was the only word that connected the thread between my sales background, my teaching, and my writing. It resonated for me, and it has stuck.

If you scroll through LinkedIn, you will see that there are many others who have adapted that storytelling title. Some complicate what that means, when it comes to business. My goal is always to simplify. That is the intent of this book.

Storytelling may seem like something that's only recently come into vogue, but it harkens back to the early days of humanity when people sat around the campfire telling tales. The basic arc of a story has not changed since then. In addition to containing a clear beginning, middle and an end—as mentioned earlier—there are five distinct elements to great storytelling:

1. Something that captivates our attention from the opening line or opening scene;
2. Setting the stage for what is to come;
3. An inciting event that piques our interest and keeps us hooked;
4. The unraveling of the story;
5. A resolution or restoring balance to life as we knew it.

A good pitch uses these same elements with one big difference. A pitch has a purpose. An author who sits down to write a work of fiction may have a great idea or start with a particular character, but they don't necessarily know where that writing will take them and how that story will end. In business we know where we want it to end. We want our audience to be as convinced as we are that what we are presenting is something they want.

A pitch is an argument for why whatever we are presenting is a great idea. Instead of being argumentative in the fighting sense, we use story to connect and get our message across persuasively.

Neuroscience research has shown evidence that good story literally changes our brain chemistry, even releasing oxytocin, that delightful feeling we get when we fall in love or eat a piece of rich, dark chocolate. That's what pulls us in and engages us. A well-told story will open our eyes so that we see a situation through the eyes of another.

While our story might be entertaining, it has a greater purpose. And we know what that purpose is going in.

The pitch also abides by a "rule" that all good writers know: *Show Me. Don't Tell Me.* None of us want to be told to do anything. But if we show someone why they should do something, if we can engage them through story, everything changes.

The Internet has enabled marketing to evolve from a push method of driving a message home through repetition to pulling our customers towards us with engaging and relevant content that show potential customers the value in whatever is offered. It's what marketers call outbound marketing versus inbound marketing.

Marketers who use digital tools like social media successfully understand that. Others continue to use the new technologies with old push methods and wonder why it's not working so well. The answer: no one wants to be told to do anything. No one. But they do want to be shown.

In similar ways, a good novel uses words to create a visual picture. A good TV show or film uses words and visuals to transport us and keep us engaged.

A good pitch creates a picture in the mind's eye with words and visuals so the audience can "see" the idea we are presenting in action. When we can get someone to visualize something that solves a problem for them, to "see" that solution, we are on our way to persuading them that what we have to offer is something they need.

PRO TIP "The best way to sell an idea is to wrap it in a story. Make it vivid, make it dramatic, and most importantly, make it visual."

—Steve Jobs

Applying The Story Arc to The Pitch

This may sound fine when writing the great American novel or the next Oscar worthy screenplay, but how does this apply to pitching a business idea? Let's look at the five storytelling elements again, with a pitch specifically in mind. There's a sixth element at the end, for your audience's added benefit.

1. Hook them from the opening line: *Get the attention of whomever you're pitching to.*
2. Set the stage: *This is the current business market situation as we know it and it includes data informed insights.*
3. The inciting event: *This is the unveiling of your brilliant idea.*
4. The unraveling of the story: *These are the details of how this idea will work.*
5. Satisfying conclusion: *Tell them what you told them and leave them interested enough to want more.*
6. The credits: *The acknowledgements for how you created this story.*

We'll go into each of these in detail in Part 2.

Using Story to Make a Point Within a Pitch

An anecdotal story can be used to drive home a key point within a pitch. For example, if I want to highlight our growing addiction to mobile devices and how it competes for our attention, within my pitch I could say exactly that. No one is going to disagree. I could even back it up with several pieces of data to validate my insights.

However, I could choose a more effective option: beginning the pitch with an anecdote about getting in the elevator to come to the meeting that day. In my story, there was one other person shooting up the floors with me: a young woman in a business suit and expensive looking shoes who did not look up from her mobile device. She clutched her phone with her well-manicured hands as if it were a precious jewel and never once lifted her eyes from the screen to notice I was there. When the doors opened and she walked off, her polished fingertips feverishly typed what I am sure was either an email to one of her staff or a critical comment on an Instagram post. I could have been holding a six-inch knife in my hand, and she would not have noticed there might be danger close by.

My anecdote is much more likely to capture my audience's attention than if I'd merely made a statement about our addiction to technology.

I am not suggesting your entire pitch be composed of personal anecdotes, but when used in the right context, they can be very effective. It's no coincidence that this book is sprinkled with my personal stories to explain various points instead of simply stating those points.

Choosing Your Tools

As you go through the process of developing a pitch, you're going to need choose a tool that allows you to visualize the framework and see how to best move the story forward . The tool, or tools, that you select should be as visual as possible and accessible to everyone involved, allowing them to make comments and notes.

Tools are a matter of preference. You can go old school and begin with a pen and a yellow legal pad, or an outline in Word. A large sketchbook along with a set of colored markers allows for visualization. You can add comments with post-it notes. Another retro option is to begin with a set of index cards, which could help you easily rearrange a sequence. If you have access to a whiteboard that no one is going to erase over the course of the process you have the added value of a larger visual space.

While all of these options suffice, none of them gives you or your team access at anytime and anywhere. That real-time access is critical when you are collaborating with team members that are in other physical locations, at least some of the time.

Crafting your pitch is a creative endeavor. And when in creative mode, ideas can pop into your head during the strangest times: when you're riding the subway, binging Netflix, or cleaning your bathroom. You want to capture those gems as they reveal themselves, before they escape into the ether. That way, you will be sure and have them at hand when you next sit down to work on your pitch. There are tools that allow for that—synching between all your devices. And if you choose the right one, collaborators can access the workspace.

There are many options that check all those boxes. Miro, a visual collaboration tool, is one that I recommend. Essentially a virtual whiteboard, it digitizes what was once only available in an analog environment. Miro can be accessed from wherever you are, on whatever device you choose. It allows you to invite other team members to share their input in real time. This particular option allows you to paste notes, comments, and links to resources, keeping everything (including your research) in one place.

When you choose a visual tool to craft your story arc from the moment you begin the process, it allows you to continually see the proverbial forest *en masse*. And hopefully, it will prevent you from knocking your head against too many of the trees along the way.

PRO TIP: "One of the most powerful things you can do to stand out from the crowd is to leverage the power of visual thinking and visual communication. When you use visual imagery and visual language, it enables you to paint a picture with words and create a mental movie in the mind's eye of your audience."

—Todd Cherches, CEO of BigBlueGumball
and Author of VisuaLeadership

What I Will Not Assume

Statements like "as we all know" or "everyone knows" make me a bit crazy. My students get tired of hearing me remind them that we don't know what anyone else knows. We can assume, but we don't really know, and we must take that into consideration when writing a pitch.

I could assume that before reading this book, you've done all the homework that is necessary to create a pitch, but I'm not going to. I don't know who you are, why you picked up this book, or what (or to whom) you're pitching.

That said, before you start crafting your pitch be sure you can answer these questions.

What are you pitching?

Whether it's an idea, a product, a service, or even you as a candidate for a job, if you're not clear on what you're pitching, you might as well stop right now and get clear on it. You can't sell something that you yourself do not fully understand.

Can you state what you're pitching in one sentence?

In the early days of the social network once known as Twitter, tweets were limited to 140 characters or less. Not only was that fun, it was also a great creative exercise that forced users to be concise with their language if they wanted to make and break through the noise.

While the length of tweets and threads eventually expanded, the idea behind the pithy post is worth practicing. Instead of limiting yourself to characters, make certain you can state the essence of the strategy behind your idea in one sentence.

In their book, *Smart Brevity, The Power of Saying More With Less,* the authors, Jim VandeHei, Mike Allen and Roy Schwartz say there is a sign that hangs on the wall of the Axios newsroom in Virginia that reads: "Brevity is confidence. Length is fear."

Being able to state our ideas succinctly is a sign that we know what they are and that we believe in them. It's also important to keep things short and to the point because our attention spans continue to shrink. A goldfish has a nine-second attention span. Humans have less.

Think about that for a moment.

Less than nine seconds.

We live in a world of constant distraction. Holding our attention is not an easy feat, which is why simplicity is key to getting our ideas across. If you can't grab someone's attention from the onset you become a non-starter.

If you are unable to state the essence of your idea and the strategy behind it in one sentence, it is likely you do not have an idea you will be able to sell. So, before you move on make sure you can do that.

Who is this idea, product, or service for?

In marketing we call this our target audience. Ask yourself the following questions:

Who is the person this idea solves a problem for?
What do they do?
Where do they live?
What do they like?
Where can we find them?

If you don't really understand who is likely to need whatever you're pitching, your pitch is over before it started.

Who are you pitching this idea, product, or service to?

People tend to forget about this part. You may have the greatest idea in the world or be the very best candidate for a job. But you'll go nowhere, fast, if you don't know who you're pitching to and cannot connect with them.

> Who is the person or persons you are pitching to?
> What is their background?
> What do you know about the company they represent?
> What is important to them?

This is not hard stuff to uncover anymore. A simple Google search or a peek at a LinkedIn profile can be very enlightening. The more we know about who we're pitching to the more likely we will be able to engage them in what we have to say.

Engagement is a popular word in marketing today. Social networks like Facebook make their money by engaging us enough to stop scrolling on our phones and click a link. True engagement is about connection. And when we pitch, we want to connect. A really effective pitch is never a monologue. It becomes a conversation.

What is the problem that you're solving?

Marketing in its pure sense is about solving problems. Businesses create products and services to answer needs. A good pitch solves a problem. Sometimes we're given a problem to tackle, and sometimes we have a new business idea that solves a problem we uncovered in our research. In some pitches, we ourselves may be the answer that's needed, because we're the best person for the job.

Who or what is the competition?

There is always competition. That is the beauty of a capitalistic society.

Who is it?

What is it?

How do you stack up against them?

What are the market conditions?

As I write this book, there are market conditions that have affected everyone no matter who they are or where they are on the planet. For example, COVID-19 has had short and long-term effects on businesses, including (but certainly not limited to) supply chain issues and increased digital consumption. There is a war raging in Ukraine that may seem distant to many reading this but has far-reaching effects for everyone. And they will continue long after the war ends. There is a shift away from traditional 9 to 5 in-office work environments, as some employers allow staff members the flexibility to work from home. There also is inflation.

All these conditions affect how we approach our business and our pitches today. Market conditions can be specific to an industry, or they can be very general. By the time you are reading this book these conditions may have changed. When that happens so may our strategy.

How does this idea, product, or service work?

Before you can start writing your pitch you must know every detail of your idea, product, or service and yet—this is key—be able to explain it as simply as possible. In marketing, this is referred to as the activation.

What action do you want your target customers to take?

What assets need to be created to interest this target and get them to take that action?

What tactics are you going to use to spark the desired response?

What resources do you need to activate this idea?

How will you measure success?

You can't manage what you can't measure. What key performance indicators (KPIs) will indicate how successful this idea will be when implemented?

How much will this cost?

No great idea comes without an expense. That said, it is always best to present your idea as an investment that will turn a good ROI (return on investment), as opposed to a budget expenditure. It's semantics, but word choice does matter in how we hear things. This is true even if you're pitching your boss for a higher salary.

Why are you pitching?

What is the reason you are crafting this pitch? If you don't know that answer, the rest becomes irrelevant.

One final note

All these questions should be answered before you begin crafting your narrative and—*this is important*—be backed by cold, hard data. Facts do matter.

PRO TIP: "I had the opportunity to work and pitch with Waggener Edstrom (WE) Co-Founder, Pam Edstrom, who passed away in 2017. She taught anyone who worked with her that you always need to ask—what is the business problem you are trying to solve. That sounds simple but even on the brand side, leaders often rush to the idea without doing the due diligence on the problem and white space ideation. It's always stuck with me and it's something I tell my team—what problem are we trying to solve."

—Nadina Guglielmetti, Chief Customer Officer, The Vitamin Shoppe

"People think in stories, not statistics, and marketers need to be master storytellers."

—Arianna Huffington

PART 2
The Framework

We've set the stage. Now it's time to take a deeper dive into each element of the story arc and how you can apply those elements when crafting your pitches.

#1 THE HOOK:
Getting the Attention of Your Audience

Back in the days when the only way to buy a book was in a physical store, I loved to wander in the Barnes & Noble that once stood at the corner of West 68th Street and Broadway in Manhattan. I would meander among the tables that were strategically dispersed throughout the five-story building for a title and cover that attracted me. When something caught my eye, I would pick the book up, open it, and start to read. I could decide within a few minutes whether or not that book was going home with me. If those first few pages didn't engage me, I knew the likelihood I would ever finish the book was minuscule and my purchase would be a waste of money.

When the first episode of "Grey's Anatomy" aired in 2005, the very first scene opened with Meredith and Derek the morning after what appeared to have been a one-night stand. We're not sure. We have a feeling this is going to be something more, but we don't know yet. It was an initial hook, one that drew me and enough other fans into a story that has engaged an audience on broadcast television since 2005. Today, it continues to engage a new, younger audience through the miracle of Netflix.

So why am I talking about books and television shows in a book about pitches?

Because the same rule applies.

If we get someone's attention from the onset, they are more likely to sit up, put away their mobile devices, and pay attention to what we have to say. Getting someone's attention and holding it in today's world of 24/7 distractions without the aid of addictive algorithms is not easy, but it is possible. It just requires creativity, doing your homework, knowing what you're about to pitch, and to whom you're pitching—inside and out.

Your hook is essentially a tease of what is to come. It's not complicated. The purpose is to draw your audience in so they will listen to whatever idea you have come up with that will help solve a problem they have and advance their business.

Just keep in mind that hooking an audience from the start only works when the information you present afterwards is worth your audience's time. What gets our attention, is not what holds it.

Boring is boring.

Every presentation is going to start with you and your team standing physically or virtually with the cover slide of your pitch as a backdrop. Try not to be mundane.

That does not mean you need to begin with a tap dance—although I suppose that could work in the right circumstance. The goal, with an introduction, is to capture your audience's interest and stimulate their curiosity. You want to signal to your audience that whatever you say next is something worth listening to.

Unfortunately, you don't have much time. Remember the goldfish. In reality you likely will have more than a precious nine seconds worth of time, but don't count on much more.

Use those first few moments to make an impression, catch the attention of your audience, and give them an indication of the effort you and your team have put into the presentation. It may appear a small detail, but the cover slide should match the essence of what the brand is—in color, style, and image. The slide is a touchpoint that will influence the audience's opinion. And it's part of the experience you are creating.

Boring never works. It does not hook us. Instead, boring makes an audience look at the clock and wonder how much time this is going to take. A boring introduction might include the sentence, "*We're here to present our idea.*" Your audience knows that part already. That is why they are in the room. Not only is it dull, but it also wastes time that could be best spent elsewhere. This is a 20-minute story you are about to tell, not a 90-minute documentary.

What works is a good hook. That hook can start with a single image.

I have a black and white picture of my eight-year-old self, dressed in my tap-dancing outfit before my first (and what would be my last) dance recital. There is a story behind that photo. And I've used it more than once to set the stage for pitches where it makes sense.

The story is of a young girl whose dance instructor told her mother after that recital that she was wasting her money on lessons and that the girl was not a dancer. The girl was crushed. She was a straight A student and until then had never failed at anything. The girl's family did not have a lot of extra money to spend, so the lessons stopped.

That girl grew up thinking she couldn't dance, that she was clumsy and awkward and too tall. She avoided dancing for years. Then one day, decades later, she met a ballroom dance instructor named Alex who told her he could teach her. She didn't believe him but wanted to, so she decided to give him her money and sign up for some lessons. It turned out Alex was right. She could dance. Alex taught her to get out of her head, let her body lead, and take the first step.

That anecdote has helped me to hook an audience when I want

them to get out of their heads—to discard all the "buts" and reasons why something is not going to work and be open to my ideas. At the same time, it demonstrates my own humanity and provides an opportunity for a point of connection with my audience.

A quote can serve as a good hook.

Just any old quote you happen to like is not going to work. The quote must be relevant to what is to follow. It should get the audience thinking, make them pause and hopefully wonder what is going to happen next. When choosing this option, the quote should be in a big and bold font on your slide and cite whoever said it.

Data can be an effective hook.

Whatever statistics you choose to use must be relevant to what will follow. It should be displayed in bold type with the proper citation. Remember a hook is a tease into what is to follow. It is not clickbait. It is far from the whole story. It is the beginning of the story.

Personal anecdotes can hook.

I used the example earlier where I combined a single image (me in a tap-dancing costume) with a personal anecdote. While that kind of story does not need an image to help you connect with audiences, a hook can be more impactful if you include one. The image behind you might be on the cover slide. What's most important is that the anecdote has something to do with the presentation that is going to follow and the journey you are about to take us on.

Questions force us to engage.

Questions are also good ways to help hook someone in as they compel people to sit up, listen, and pay attention. When I am speaking about personal branding, I often start by asking what that term means to my audience. Something as simple as requiring someone to raise their hand engages them physically and encourages them to wonder what's coming next. At the same time, the physical response gives me an indication of what my audience thinks and invites their participation. My goal at this juncture is to get their attention by encouraging them to take part in the conversation.

A hook does not need to be fancy.

High tech introductions can dazzle and be effective in many instances—depending on who you are pitching to, but it is not necessary for a solid hook. Instead, clarity and intrigue are of ultimate importance. Whether it is three words on a slide or a high-definition video, your hook is an invitation that you have something to say that is worthy of your audience's time. It should give some indication of what is to follow without fast-forwarding to your big idea. You want this to be just enough of a tease to make your audience want to listen to what else you have to say.

Above all the hook should be relevant to the story that is about to unfold.

TRY THIS: Watch a TED Talk. One of my favorites features Tricia Wang, an ethnographer and cofounder of Sudden Compass, who speaks on the human insights missing from big data. After watching, answer the following:

- What hook did the speaker use to pull you in?
- Why did it work?

Do one more thing.

After hooking an audience, there is another thing you need to do before you start unfolding your story: introduce yourself and your team. This should be short but sweet. Have fun with it. Show your human side. Portray yourself and your team as people not only as qualified but people whose values align with the audience's and who they might want to do business with. Remember: your homework is not just research on a given company, but on who you are presenting to.

As we move into Web3, many of us want to immerse ourselves into the Metaverse, a vision of virtual worlds that are "peopled" by avatars and require VR headsets designed to mimic reality. There's no doubt that the metaverse deserves attention, especially as GenZ—a generation raised on mobile devices, gaming, and social media—is coming of age. At the same time, there is no doubt that the human species is hardwired to connect with other living, breathing beings.

There will undoubtedly be a point in the future where you will be presenting in a metaverse, just as we have found ourselves engaging virtually on Zoom or a hybrid of Zoom and in-person.

However, what won't change and has not changed since the beginning of time is our desire to make a human connection. We want to work with people we know something about, who we think are qualified to help us and who can differentiate themselves from artificial intelligence.

TRY THIS: Answer these questions, in preparation for introducing yourself to an audience:
- Who are you?
- What titles do you use?
- Why are you qualified to help?

This may sound easy, but these are challenging questions—even for the most experienced.

#2 SETTING THE STAGE:
Problem and Insights

Before we can introduce our wonderful solution to the problem in question, we have to set the stage for your story. This includes:

- A statement of the problem that includes a brief recap of what we know about the brand and the brand's current situation.
- The insights we learned from the research we have done that led us to our big idea.

Let's look at each one.

The Statement of the Problem

All pitches solve a problem.

In marketing, we are often given problems to solve by our clients. Sometimes pitches uncover problems, or needs, that no one knew they had, and we offer up some solutions. That's what happened when Steve Jobs introduced the iPhone in 2007. No one knew this new device would soon become an indispensable part of our everyday lives.

As you begin to set the stage of your story, you want to state the problem clearly and succinctly in one sentence. Not two or three sentences or 300 words.

One sentence.

This is an important kick-off point. Even when we've been given a problem to solve by a client, we can never, never, never assume that the client will remember exactly what the assignment was.

Even when they do, we have no idea what kind of a day they've had or what is going on in their lives that might be distracting. We don't know if they slept the night before; if their dog is at the vet; or if they just had a challenging conversation with their boss. We might even be surprised to find that the meeting includes people we weren't expecting, and they don't have much information about its purpose. All we know is that we want to get their attention and we want to hold it.

A clear, concise statement of the problem explains why they need to pay attention. It allows our audience to focus and reminds them that we know what the problem is, and we are here to offer a solution.

PRO TIP: "You're not the first nor the last pitch your client has heard or will ever hear. Stand apart. Be the outlier, the one and only pitch that was memorable."

—Bill Lee, Servant Leader and Go to Market Expert
(formerly at Samsung, Nickelodeon, and Sony)

The Current Situation

Trust is hard to come by these days. According to the 2022 Edelman study trust is at an all-time low. We are skeptical of the media, the government, and thanks to the spread of misinformation and disinformation on social networks, often each other.

Setting the stage is about building trust. We do that by presenting evidence that we understand:

- What the brand is and what the goals are;
- What the market is they are trying to reach;
- The problem we are solving for them;
- The goals they want to achieve;
- The current market conditions that may be impacting the brand.

That may sound like a lot to cover in a limited amount of time but believe it or not the above can be stated in one to two sentences.

When we offer evidence that we have done our homework we gain authority. It demonstrates that we care about their business and want to help it grow. We show proof that the idea we're about to present was not pulled out of thin air, with no data to back it up.

If we show up as if we are just there for the money, we build no trust and risk falling into the stereotypical pitch man who bears a resemblance to Alec Baldwin's classic character in 1992 in "Glengarry Glen Ross"—the type of salesperson that makes people cringe at the word "sell."

Again, brevity is critical. You're here to sell an idea and use story to do that. Every single section of your pitch should support that as simply as possible. When we confuse, we lose.

TRY THIS: Choose a pitch that you are either working on right now, have worked on previously, or plan to work on soon. Fill in the following blanks:

- The brand and what they do _____
- The problem that needs to be solved _____
- The goals the brand wants to achieve _____
- The marketplace realities _____

Based on this understanding, you can present an idea that solves a problem, with insights that back up your solution—in one sentence!

Insights—Not Data

It's estimated that we produce 2.5 quintillion bytes of data every day. We're drowning in it. We're obsessed with it.

Data-driven technologies. Data-driven innovation. Data-driven... blah, blah, blah.

I'm all for data. I believe in it. Statistics are necessary to understand and solve problems. We need it to make a convincing argument. All that research you did in coming up with your idea gave you mountains of information. But data alone are just a bunch of numbers on a chart.

The phrase "data-driven" implies data is driving the train and data is all that matters. That could not be farther from the truth. Instead, the story behind the numbers gives us what's essential to our pitch. In other words, the story comes from what we learned from the data and the insights that it gave us. That's how you set the stage.

The insights become clues that lead us to a fantastic idea. In an effective pitch, insights are sprinkled like breadcrumbs leading to our great idea. When we unveil that revelation, the initial hook, at the start of the pitch, begins to make sense.

Data does not tell our story; it informs our story and supports our argument. We want it to validate our idea, making it powerful and impactful. By itself, without the insights we have learned from data, our idea lacks credibility. It means nothing.

As you set the stage you want to present three key insights that you learned from your research that led you to the big idea you are about to present.

Three. Remember the rule of three discussed in Part One.

Insights are not data. Insights are what you learned from the data. Each of the three insights should be supported by data that is sourced. A good rule of thumb is that each insight should have three pieces of data cited that supports it.

Insights help to advance your story. They help explain why your idea is a good one. The more visually you present your insights, the more impact they will have.

Use a key piece of data to prove the point you want to make. Because it supports your insight, present that piece of data as boldly as you can. Position the data's source like a footnote, in the bottom right corner of your slide. That will help avoid distractions. You want your audience to pay attention to you, not the nitty gritty. If a full chart is called for, save it for the Appendix.

PRO TIP: "Stories carry the emotion; data supports that story."

—Robert McKee, Author, Story Mentor

#3 THE INCITING EVENT:
Your Big Idea

The inciting event is the moment in any story when the stakes have been raised and things change. You've held our interest to this point. If you've done that effectively, we're committed and want to know what happens next.

In the case of a pitch, the inciting event is when you pull back the curtain and unveil your big idea. When done right, this is the moment when your audience starts to understand where you were going when you set the stage with your insights. The goal is to make them sit at the edge of their chair, anxious to hear what comes next.

Your idea has a name. The strategy behind this idea can be stated in one sentence.

Not two or three.

Not a paragraph.

One sentence.

Your sentence is clear and succinct. It interests us (the audience) enough to keep listening.

This is a crucial point in any pitch. If we have to think too much, you have lost us. There are dozens of stories in the naked city about clients who steal glances at their Apple watches at this point. Or they start scrolling their smartphones, say they've heard enough, stand up and leave the room.

But they won't go anywhere if you demonstrate that you understand their business and provide insights backed by credible data that shows how your idea can solve our problem. They'll still be listening.

PRO TIP: "The best ideas are simple ideas."

—David Ogilvy, Founder of Ogilvy and Mather,
considered the "Father of Advertising"

#4 THE UNRAVELING OF YOUR STORY:
How This Works

We haven't left the room yet, but that does not mean you've sold us on anything. All it means is that you have told us enough to hold our interest. Explaining the details of how your brilliant idea works can get tricky. Unfortunately, this is where you can really lose a crowd.

You want to show us that you have thought through all the details, but you don't want to get so lost in those details that we forget what the idea is and cannot make sense of how this is going to help our business.

It is very easy when explaining how an idea works to get caught up in the tactics of how this idea can come to life. When that happens, you lose sight of the problem you are there to solve and how your idea satisfies the overall business objectives of the brand. In other words, how this is going to make money.

Instead, continue to take us on the journey you started when you hooked us into the story. This section can be thought of as subplot or a story within your story. You have a wonderful idea and now you are going to walk us through the details, step by step, as if we are the customer. The challenge is to accomplish that as simply as possible— which sounds much easier than it is.

The more you can show us, instead of telling us, the more effective and attention-holding this part of your pitch will be. The more visual you can make this section, the more impactful it becomes.

You want to create an idea in your audience's mind so they can "see" not just what is physically put in front of them, but the larger picture. Presenting relevant visuals as you take them on the journey— step by step, as simply as possible—is an effective way to do that.

I am going to say that again. *As. Simply. As. Possible.* When you confuse us, you lose us. As you plan out how to do this, be crystal clear on what the overall business goal is, what CTA (call to action) you want your target customer to take, and how you will get them to take it.

Think through every little detail of how you will execute this. You should be able to answer every possible question your client might ask, but you do not, and *I repeat*, do not want to list every minuscule detail on your slides.

When you force us to read, you lose our attention. Always remember that you and your team are the stars of this pitch. You are the one taking us on this journey, not your pitch deck. The pitch deck is there to enhance what you say, not detract from it, and to remind you (as the presenter) where you are in the storytelling so you don't get off track.

Don't just tell us about an idea for new content. Instead, create a video, or sizzle reel, that gives a "taste" of what it will be like.

Don't tell us what images you are going to use on Instagram. Show us what that Instagram post would look like.

Don't tell us what happens when a customer gets to a landing page. Mock-up that landing page, so we can see exactly what the customer will see. This can often be a very effective way to depict the activation of your idea.

Don't tell us what the in-store interactive experience will be. Create a visual that mocks up what it would look like.

Don't tell us you will pay influencers to promote your marketing idea. Find the influencers that make sense for the brand and the idea. Show us who they are.

Don't tell us you plan for podcast advertising. Choose the podcasts that make the best sense to this particular idea and tell us why you selected them.

When Steve Jobs stood on a stage at Macworld on Jan. 9, 2007, and introduced the world to the iPhone he did not throw up a bunch of bullet points on a slide and say, "Here it is. The iPhone. Go buy it." Instead, he used intrigue, humor, and images. He showed us how it would change the world. Once he showed us this revolutionary new device, he continued to sell us, introducing each and every one of the features. He held our attention, and he sold us.

As you take us on your journey, that is what you should do. You want to show us more than the details of your fabulous idea, you want to continually reinforce why this solution to a problem matters.

Never assume that whoever is sitting in front of you is going to figure that out by themselves. Your job is to lead them to that conclusion through effective storytelling.

This is also known as selling – that dirty word we talked about reframing in Part 1.

PRO TIP: "Think about the problem you're solving for the person you're pitching to and focus on the end benefit to that person. Bad pitches are usually focused on the product or process and not on the needs of the audience being pitched."

—David Vinjamuri, President, Thirdway Brand Trainers

How You Will Measure

Getting a good grade is something that is drilled into our heads from the moment we start school. The competition starts early. We want to know how we did relative to our classmates.

A similar measurement process will happen if your client signs on to the idea you've pitched. They're going to want to determine its success based on the original business objective. Those outcomes could be compared to their own past performance or to that of the competition. This process is part of the unraveling of your story. You will need to identify what those KPIs (key performance indicators) should be and the benchmarks that you think should be set to measure that success.

Keep. It. Simple.

When Stephen D. Rappaport wrote "The Digital Metrics Field Guide" in 2015, he identified 350 metrics, which he whittled done to 197 for the book. That was just for digital marketing.

In the years since, what we can measure has grown exponentially not just in digital marketing—where we can measure everything from sentiment to changes in behavior to a lift in revenue—but in any area your pitch might fall under. Technology has enabled this. Your job is to identify three KPIs that will best measure the success of your idea.

Three. Once again, the magic number.

That is not to say there will be only three metrics you can look at to gauge the idea's success. There is always something more to look at that might be helpful to your client's business. That is something the analytics team will dive into after the idea is activated. However, for the pitch, your job is to simplify the complex and decide which three KPIs will best relate to your idea and to the larger business objective in order to measure its success.

For example, brand awareness is often a business goal, but it is also very general. If brand awareness is the larger objective, your job is to determine what three KPIs that specifically relate to brand awareness you can measure that is most relevant for your idea.

In his book, "The Hype Machine," Sinan Aral addresses the importance of lift in measurement. He defines lift as a change in behavior from what the targeted customer would ordinarily do. Behavior metrics may be the best KPIs to measure the success of your idea.

Choosing a specific number for your KPIs is like trying to hit the bullseye on a dart board. It's possible, but it's not easy. The odds are against you, if you predict that one specific number will be reached. Instead, choose your target KPIs as ranges or percentages. That also allows for unanticipated events or circumstances that might affect your success rate.

No matter what your idea or what KPIs you present, someone in the room is going to want to know how your idea is going to make them money. Whether the idea offers a solution that is a direct or indirect line to revenue does not matter. What does matter is that you should be prepared to answer that question.

PRO TIP: "The most important part of the pitch happens before the meeting. You have to go in with a good understanding of the person or organization you are pitching and know and appreciate the value of the product, service, or idea."
—Matthew Sawyer, Founder USAccelerator and Adjunct Professor at NYU and Columbia University.

The Investment

Everything costs money. Your idea is no different. You may have been given a budget and have based your idea and strategy around working within it. If you haven't been given a number in advance or if you are presenting a brand-new business idea, your pitch must justify why this idea is worth spending money on and how much that will be. Depending on what you are presenting you may need to include projected revenue as a justification for the investment needed to bring this idea to life.

In any of these scenarios you want to present this part of the unraveling of your story as an investment, not an expenditure. It may sound like nothing more than semantics, but word choice does matter.

An investment implies an ROI (return on investment), whereas budget or cost just sounds like we're spending money without any specific value in return. Remember: from the start of this pitch you have been taking your audience on a journey to prove why your idea is a good one and how it will solve their problem. You have been selling your audience on why your idea is worth their money and time. Now you are telling them how much of an investment they need as you continue to convince them it will be worth it.

It's important to research and think through every single expenditure—from the estimated cost of an influencer to the video content that needs to be created to the estimated price for building a pop-up store. A spreadsheet will be necessary. However, spreadsheets are ugly, and you don't want ugly to intrude on the storytelling journey. Ugly sits in the Appendix.

Once again, a visual depiction is what works best. I personally prefer pie charts. They're easy to create and easy to view at a glance. They can keep the conversation moving forward and focused on your brilliant idea and why it will help achieve their business objectives and make the company money.

Save the spreadsheet along with any other detailed data or "ugly" slides for the Appendix and as a resource to pull from if and when you need to.

Depending on the pitch and who is in the room, you may get quizzed on these numbers and how you got to them. Be prepared to answer, letting the audience know where that detail can be found. Questions at this juncture and throughout your pitch are good signs. They provide an opportunity to make your pitch more of a conversation. They are usually an indication that not only have you created interest, but things are moving in the right direction.

PRO TIP: "What you want to say needs to be heard, so listen with all your senses when pitching. Make how you listen as important as what you have to say."

—J. Kelly Hoey, *Author of Build Your Dream Network: Forging Powerful Relationships In A Hyper-Connected World.*

#5 RESTORING BALANCE:
Tell Us What You Told Us

You've taken us (the audience) on a journey. If you've done your job well, not only have you presented a worthwhile idea, but you have also engaged us, held our interest, and persuaded us that at the very least we should seriously consider this idea for our business.

However, you can't just drop us off at the curb and say good-bye like this is the end of a bad date. As is true in any well-written story, you want to restore balance and give us a sense of resolution. In the case of a business pitch, you want to tell us what you told us.

That may sound repetitive but remember one of the great pieces of advice for any pitch is to tell us what you are going to tell us, tell us, and then tell us what you told us.

In other words, sell us one more time by summarizing what your idea is and how the execution of your strategy is going to achieve our business goals. Never, ever assume that your audience got it the first time. Remember, we are living in a world of distractions and even when you deliver a brilliant presentation, not everyone was fully paying attention every step of the way.

Features and benefits may sound a bit old school, but if you think this part through with that in mind as your model, it can be very effective in crafting this part of your story.

For example, try filling in these blanks. A feature of this idea is _____ and this is how it benefits your business _____.

A feature by itself means absolutely nothing if you do not point out and reinforce in no uncertain terms how it solves your client's problem.

Consider this scenario: a potential graduate student is considering applying to NYU's School of Professional Studies. If the student asked someone to comment on its features, the person responding might say that NYU is a world-renowned university, with a noted and reputable practitioner faculty, and it sits in the heart of a world class city.

These are all nice features. However they don't specifically explain why they matter to the student applying. The benefits of these features do that.

For example, NYU is a recognized university across the globe, which means that the value of the degree you receive from NYU precedes itself. Because faculty members are practitioners, students learn not just theory, but practical real-world applications that will make them better prepared for their chosen career path. The fact that it sits in the heart of New York City means that in addition to an education, attendees have easy access to art, theater, music, and museums.

Note that you do not need to use the words feature and benefit as you establish each one. I've stated it like this to give you a starting point. Remember, crafting a pitch is a creative endeavor. Everything should be custom-tailored to you, the audience you are presenting to, and your idea.

Once again, I suggest using the number three. If you are unable to come up with three features of your idea and a reason for each that explains why this is going to achieve the business objective, you have not done your job. In that case you need to go back and work on the idea itself and/or how you are presenting it.

PRO TIP: "One of the biggest mistakes people make when pitching is focusing on features instead of benefits and values. The thing is features are always about you and your product or idea. However, to create a connection and generate interest you must talk about what matters to your audience, the benefits and the value they get."

—Dr. Maria Blekher, Board Member, Early Stage Investor,
Behavioral Scientist

Ask for the Order

Less than a year into my first job selling country music radio ads, I went to a Hank Williams, Jr. concert in Kennett Square, Pennsylvania with the staff. After several cocktails, my sales manager and general manager pulled me aside and basically told me that I had to pick up the pace or I was not going to make it. They told me I had everything going for me to be a successful sales executive, but I just wasn't closing anything, and in sales you are only as good as your last order. They had noticed that I got the appointments, got the second and third calls, clients liked me, but I wasn't getting the deal done.

In today's world there are probably a dozen human resource rules that would prohibit such a conversation at an after-work country music concert when alcohol was involved and with no documentation, but this was the '80s. It was a different time. However questionable the approach might seem in today's world, it worked.

I needed to be told in no uncertain terms what I was doing and what I wasn't doing. I needed to decide how I was going to change that—or else I was going to find myself unemployed. It was what I like to call "tough love." My managers wanted me to succeed, but knew they had to tell me what I did not want to hear. This was no time for coddling or worrying about hurt feelings. It had to be done if I had any chance of success.

The problem was, I wasn't asking for the order. I moved the deals forward, but when it came to closing, I choked. I was afraid of getting a no, so to avoid that I didn't ask. Instead, I chose to hope that someday, somehow the deal might close, rather than trying to close it. That is not sustainable in the business world.

I hadn't yet learned that a no is better than a maybe. A no opens the door to improving an idea so eventually it does get closed, or it allows you to let go and move on. A no allows you to ask why, and that answer can give you information to turn the pitch around with that potential client. Or it can be used to improve a pitch in the future.

A maybe leaves you in limbo. A maybe dangling out there in the ether is just a wish that maybe, maybe, maybe someday in the future the deal will close.

As someone who had no intention of failing in my selling career, I pushed myself to get past my fear of hearing that dreaded no and started asking for the order. It was a simple fix, and it worked. A yes brought elation, a no, not so much. But when there was a no, I could ask why and either see if I could fix it or let that one go, learn from it, and move on.

This is the point in the resolution of your pitch when you need to ask for the business. You may not get the answer you want, but you will get an answer. From there you can determine what next steps need to be taken. If you don't ask, you don't get. It's that simple.

TRY THIS: Practice asking. Start small. Ask a question in a meeting. Ask your waiter to explain something on the menu. Ask for what you want.

#6 THE CREDITS:
The Appendix

The end of any good story includes the credits. In a novel, the author will acknowledge all the people that helped them to write, polish, and eventually publish that book. After the last scene in a film, we see a screen roll of the credits that tell us who was responsible for what, citing all the people and organizations who helped to create the finished product.

In the case of a pitch, the Appendix is your screen roll. It includes a summary of the references you used in your research that led to your idea. It substantiates that you did not make up any of the data cited.

This might include the full graph from a piece of the data you included in your Insights section, links to those references, or the articles you used in your research.

The Appendix is where you would also include a detailed spreadsheet of the costs associated with implementing this idea, which you touched on in the Investment section.

You could even go so far as to include a contract to cement the deal, but that would depend on where in the process this particular pitch sits.

In short, the Appendix is where everything that looks ugly on a slide goes, anything that is so detailed it would force us to read instead of listening to you.

The Appendix is there for your audience, and it is also there for you to point to and refer to if needed.

"I have never worked a day in my life without selling. If I believe in something, I sell it, and I sell it hard."

—Estée Lauder

PART 3
It's Not Enough to Know Your Story, You Have to Sell it

You've done your research. You've established the insights you learned from the data. Those insights have led you to an idea you are convinced is going to work. You know how this idea will be activated. You've outlined the story arc of your pitch. Now it's time to pull it all together and craft a concise, convincing, and engaging pitch that holds attention and that can be told in 20 minutes.

Your slide deck serves to enhance that pitch, but it will not tell the story completely. You and your team, if you are working with one, will. You are not writing a book or a graduate thesis, you are creating a slide deck that supports the story arc of the presentation you have crafted.

The stars of this show are not the slides. You are. No matter how fancy or glossy they look, no matter what special effects are incorporated into your presentations, the slides do not sell your idea. You do.

In this section, we'll discuss how to use the slide deck so it does not use you. And I'll also give some other tips on how to deliver a more effective presentation.

Designing Your Slides

Charles Eames, a noted industrial designer—most famous for the Eames chair he co-created with Ray Eames—once said: "Design is a plan for arranging the elements in a way that best accomplishes a particular purpose."

Now that you have the framework for your pitch, your slides should be designed with that in mind. It should match the flow of the story arc you have created to show how you are solving your client's problem. The following are suggestions for each slide based on the story arc that was discussed in Part 2.

Once again remember, this book is a framework, not a template. That means creativity is encouraged. You can custom tailor this framework to best fit your brand, the circumstances, and your idea as long as it maintains the arc of the story you are telling: hook – problem – insights - the idea – details how the idea works - measurement – investment - conclusion - ask.

#1 The Hook – Your Introduction

As you present your hook, you'll need two slides.

- Cover slide
- Introduction of your team

71

A slide that says "This is a Presentation for Your Business" is boring. It's not going to get anyone's attention. Think of this slide as the backdrop for the hook that we discussed in Part 2, keeping in mind that this is your audience's first impression of this meeting.

You may have met your audience before. You may not have. In either case introduce or reintroduce your team using pictures, names, and titles. This helps to lend credibility and establish why you are uniquely qualified to help their business.

#2 The Setting – The Problem and the Insights

In this section you'll need a minimum of four slides.

- Slide #1. Restate the problem or ASK as you understand it for the brand and explain that you are here to offer the client a soon-to-be-revealed solution. This should be done in one sentence as we discussed in Part 2.
- Slides #2-4. A minimum of three insights on one slide each.

A restatement of the problem you are solving is necessary to remind everyone of why they are there. In a world in which we are inundated with noise 24/7 we can never assume that anyone remembers anything. Again, this should be one sentence on one slide. Clean and easy to understand.

Following this will be the insights from your research that led you to the fantastic idea you are about to present. As noted, each insight should be on a separate slide. The insights should be big and bold and not require us (the audience) to think very much. Instead they will make us pause and keep us intrigued enough to wonder where you are going next in this pitch.

The full citation for the data that helped you to glean these insights should be in the Appendix, however a small citation should also be noted in the bottom right-hand corner of the corresponding slide. That helps to build credibility and trust and tells us that you have done your homework.

#3 The Inciting Event - Your Big Idea

One slide is sufficient to give your audience a big Ta da! moment. This is when you pull the curtains back and reveal your brilliant idea! Everything you have shown us so far has led to this, so give us a chance to pause and take it in.

That single slide can be as simple as one sentence that tells us what the idea is. Or it can be as elaborate as a video that you created. It all depends on who you are pitching and what your idea is.

What is critical here is that the idea is easily understood. No one should be forced to think too hard to figure out what you mean. They get it, and they are ready to hear more.

#4 The Unraveling of the Story—How This Works

The number of slides required will vary, depending on your idea. It is possible to explain an idea in as few as three well-designed and easy-to-follow slides. However depending on what the idea is, that may not be feasible. Regardless, it's essential that the point of each slide is conveyed without forcing anyone to think too hard.

Remember this is where many presenters forget they are selling an idea. When that happens, you can easily lose the interest and engagement of your audience by making the execution too complicated and too hard to follow. The slides are there to help simplify things, not complicate them.

#5 The KPIs

You are not selling the KPIs you have identified to measure the success of the idea you have presented, but they are necessary to move this narrative forward. It is possible that one slide that is easy to read will be sufficient, however a slide for each KPI can also work.

What is key is that the KPIs are easy to understand at a glance, and you can explain how they reflect back to the business objective. Once again, you are selling the idea, not the KPIs so you don't want to linger here too long.

#6 The Investment

One slide with a visual depiction of the investment should be all that's necessary.

No spreadsheet anywhere ever looked good projected on a flat screen. Leave the spreadsheet for the Appendix and refer to it when you need to.

Within the pitch itself, use a visual depiction. As mentioned earlier, my preference is always a pie chart that is labeled with the resources and assets needed to execute the idea and the percentage of the total investment for each.

Some pitches may necessitate an explanation of anticipated revenue. Again, keep it simple and visual with the spreadsheet details available in the Appendix.

Never forget you are selling your idea. What it would cost to go to market is very important, but all we need to see on this slide is enough to show where the client's money is going and/or how much money this idea could generate. If your audience is really interested, they will ask more questions and you will have those details easy to access in the Appendix. You have practiced so you will be prepared for the questions. Like many things in life, when we really like something and see the value in it, we suddenly find the money for it.

#7 Restoring the Balance—The Conclusion

This involves two slides:

- Slide #1. Lists three reasons why this idea will work;
- Slide #2. Asks for the business;

That first slide should summarize a minimum of three valid reasons why the features of this idea are going to help the client achieve its business objective. If you can't come up with three solid reasons, you need to revisit the idea and determine why.

You want to wrap up this section with a slide stating your Ask. It can be as simple as when can we start?

#8 The Credits

The number of slides in this Appendix section will vary.

All the stuff that looks ugly on the slides, that forces us to read instead of listen goes here. It should include details from your research, the investment spreadsheet, as well as any other supportive materials that prove you did not make this up.

Avoid Death by Deck

Many people more famous and influential than I am have advised presenters to ditch the slide deck completely. While that is a nice idea, the reality is that we don't want to throw the PowerPoint deck into the virtual trash can, never to be seen again.

We have increasingly become a visual society. The use of the visuals can help to make our pitches more effective. That means that instead of pressing the delete tab on our decks we need to learn how to use our decks more effectively, so they help us state an argument instead of hindering it. We want to control the slide deck, not have the slide deck control us.

Keep. It. Simple.

You are, no doubt, tired of hearing me say those words. But simplicity is the surest route to convincing an audience. Your idea may be complex. But keeping it simple refers to how you make that complexity easy to understand. Complex slides will confuse. Simple, well-designed slides will help to persuade.

Show me. Don't tell me.

You have also heard me say this, but I will say it again. Your slides should show us the argument you are making, not tell us. A slide that is full of text forces us to read. If we are busy reading, we are not paying attention to who is speaking. The result is a less effective pitch.

Each slide should advance your story and help create not only a literal picture but a visual picture in your audience's mind, showing how this idea works and how it helps their business.

Less is more.

One question I often get from my graduate students is how many slides a good pitch needs to have. My answer is always the same. It depends.

It depends on how you can best tell your story.

A good pitch could be six slides or 60. It depends on the idea and how you like to present. I use my slides as personal notecards, so I don't forget where I am in my story. The framework I have suggested in this book would require a minimum of 12 slides.

Scott Galloway, a serial entrepreneur, co-host of the "Pivot" podcast, and an NYU professor, is known for running through over 100 slides in a 40-minute presentation. It is not the number that convinces his audiences; it's how he uses them. They are visually appealing, and each one supports the points he discusses.

Most importantly, focus on how the slides are aiding you in telling an engaging story that will persuade your audience.

Remember, slides do not cost anything. You are not printing paper so there is no need to worry about killing trees. More slides with a small amount of information is always better than fewer slides crowded with text.

White space is a good thing.

In a world of perpetual distractions, every waking moment is consumed with something that shifts our attention. The tendency is to do that with our slides. We want to fill every single space on a slide with a word or image.

Don't.

If you do that, your audience spends precious time reading the slides, trying to determine what to focus on. They are not listening to you. And when they stop listening, you have lost their attention. You might as well pack up and leave the meeting right then and there.

Each slide should advance your story arc.

Each slide has a purpose that advances your story. Whatever is on that slide should help to support and reinforce your argument and yes—here comes that dirty word again—sell your idea. It should be impactful, make the audience pause and wonder where you are going with this. There should be just enough on the slide to maintain their interest.

A slide stating that adults spent one hour and 15 minutes daily using social media in 2023 in large bold type is much more impactful than flashing the eMarketer chart where you got the data. That chart and the details of the research belong in the Appendix.

Slides should match the brand essence.

Your slides should reflect the style, color, and feel of the brand and idea you are pitching. It may sound so simple, but attention to details like this demonstrate that you really understand what the brand is and that you have done your homework. It will also be more aesthetically pleasing to your audience; they will be more likely to relate to your idea and visualize their brand implementing it.

Number your slides.

Sometimes during a presentation you will experience interruptions. Personally, I like being interrupted and often invite it as my pitch becomes more conversational. It also allows me to troubleshoot objections and/or pull in other pertinent information to help my argument based on what is happening in real time.

Sometimes a client will let you finish and take notes along the way. That is when numbering comes in handy. They can jot down the number of the slide they want to question, and it allows you to quickly find the slide they are referring to.

PowerPoint is generic. There are other options.

Somewhere along the line, PowerPoint became synonymous with slide deck. However that is not your only option. I personally prefer Keynote, as I find it easier to use, but there are all sorts of options out there that can provide beautiful and professional looking templates for decks, including Canva and Google Slides. It also helps when you are lucky enough to have someone skilled in graphic design on your team.

> **PITCH POINTER:** The true showstoppers do not rely on PowerPoint. Their slides serve as cue cards to remind them where they are in the story they're telling.

Killing Your Darlings

Stephen King has been quoted as saying, "Kill your darlings, kill your darlings, even when it breaks your egocentric little scribbler's heart, kill your darlings." However, he was not the first to offer this advice to writers. A version of this wisdom has been offered by many successful writers, from Oscar Wilde to William Faulkner. The earliest version is said to date to 1916 when Sir Arthur Quiller-Couch suggested writers "murder your darlings."

If you have never heard this expression before it may at first sound a bit baffling. What could they possibly mean by advising a writer to kill or murder their darlings?

The answer is simple. Writers can get overly attached to their words. There might be a particular sentence or scene that they find impossible to discard, even if that string of words is not advancing the story line or takes it in an unnecessary direction. When that happens, the only solution is to kill it.

That's a lot easier said than done.

Letting go of what we love is not easy in any aspect of our lives. That is true when writing a story. It also holds true when creating a pitch, because we have a limited amount of time to present.

So how do you know what is necessary and what is bogging things down?

TRY THIS: Go through your pitch deck, remembering that each slide is there to advance your story and draw your audience toward a satisfying conclusion—just like each word you utter. After each slide, each sentence you plan to speak, ask yourself these questions:

- *So what?*
- *Who cares?*
- *Why does this matter to the audience I am pitching to?*
- *How does this help their business?*

The answers to those questions will help you decide what parts are necessary to prove your idea is viable, and which parts need to go. They will help you to refine and polish both your idea and your pitch. Maybe you don't have to kill a whole slide, maybe just some text on it. Maybe the slide is just perfect, but you need to improve what you are saying as that slide appears.

Outside Eyes

A good story is rarely written by one person sitting in a basement somewhere who turns out a perfectly written novel without the input of others. Outside eyes are necessary. Writers form writing groups to get feedback and help them figure out what to kill and sometimes what needs to be added in. There are editors employed to eliminate unnecessary words and improve sentence structure.

People who are not involved in writing a particular story can give perspective that the storyteller didn't consider, because they are knee deep in the weeds of the endeavor.

The same is true for your pitch. Get outside perspective on your work, preferably from people who have not been involved in the process. Test your pitch on them and ask for honest feedback. Not only will that help kill your darlings, it will also help you realize what your pitch still needs.

When I teach my NYU Real-World classes, I always invite guest judges in for a "dress rehearsal" for exactly this reason. At that point in the semester, I have seen the ideas evolve and the pitches practiced many times. I am as deeply invested as the students, and there might be something that I have missed. I want them to get a fresh set of eyes, so they know exactly what needs to be polished and perfected in that last week.

PRO TIP: "Make your words unforgettable Whether it's sharing valuable information, solving a problem, lending a listening ear or respectfully giving space, aim to be exceptionally memorable."

—George Benaroya, Global CFO

Teamwork

Nothing great was ever created in a vacuum. The majority of the pitches you will create and present will be a team effort. Sometimes you get to choose your team, and sometimes it's chosen for you. Your team may blend together seamlessly, or it may take some effort before the members work in unison.

I've found myself in both situations. Teams have challenged me, and they will challenge you. There are plenty of books out there on team building and while that is not the purpose of this one, a strong team is necessary to create and deliver an effective pitch. So I will share what has worked for me.

Despite the polarization that infiltrates the media on a daily basis, the truth is we are more alike than we are different. We just need to take a moment or two to find those points of connection with each other. In other words we need to get to know each other as human beings.

There is an exercise I use in all my classes to open the semester. Students are paired off. Each one takes a turn asking the other where they are from and then listens for three minutes. They are trying to find points of connection. When they are done each pair introduces their partner to the class, sharing not just their name and where they are from, but what engaged them most about their conversation.

No matter how many times I have asked my students to do this, I am amazed by what comes up. Students who live on the other side of the globe will learn they are from the same hometown. Others who grew up in different countries will find a shared passion for ballroom dancing or snowboarding.

When working on a team this can be followed by a second set of questions, with each person sharing what they believe they bring to the group. Owning our strengths can be challenging to say out loud but necessary. When each team member is playing to their individual strengths the result is a more effective and well-functioning team, one in which each member will appreciate the strengths of their teammates and learn from them.

I do not profess to know the intricacies of baseball, but I do know there are nine players on a baseball team and each one plays a specific position. The pitcher on the mound is not going to win a game all by himself or herself. Every one of the nine players has a specific and important role, and each team member needs to communicate with each other, even when they are not actually speaking. When the whole team shows up and does their part, the chances of playing a good game and of winning increase. And when they do not the team suffers.

Listen to what your teammates are saying when it's their turn. If you see them stumble, help them. You have heard their part as much as you have practiced your own, so you know what to say. Have each other's backs. Big pitches are rarely solo endeavors.

Like any relationship even the most successful teams will have their moments when it all falls apart. There will be ups and downs and times when you think you will never have a finished product. There will be times when you want to scream at another member of your team—or yourself. In fact, you may scream, at which point you'll need to take a breath, regroup, and work through it. That is, if your goal is a winning pitch.

PITCH POINTER: Kick off your project with an outing—anything from a group dinner to a bowling night. Whatever works for the team. Getting to know each of the other members beyond what they bring to the professional situation is the first step towards a well-functioning team.

Think "Yes," *and* Not "Yes, *but*"

Rebecca Stuard is an actor and Executive Director at Improvolution where she teaches improvisation. She is also a personal friend who one day cajoled me into taking one of her classes. Until then, I had no idea what any of the techniques of improvisation were, but I did know that they were no longer reserved for the likes of aspiring cast members on "Saturday Night Live" and that they were used in business settings for problem solving, team building, and learning to think on one's feet.

The night of the class, I found myself in a windowless upstairs studio on New York's Cornelia Street standing in a circle with the rest of the class listening to Rebecca cheerfully lead us through a "yes, and" exercise. She started by turning to the person to her right, looking them directly in their eyes and offering a story prompt. The person she was speaking to would then turn to their right, face the next person, look them directly in the eyes and say, "Yes, and." Then add one word to the story. Not two words or three or a sentence. Just one word. The instructions were to continue this as a group until she told us to stop. If that sounds easy, it wasn't, at least not for me.

I decided I knew how this story would best evolve. I would add my word and then become disappointed because the person after me would never add the word I thought they should, nor did the one after

89

them. I wanted to control the story flow, but I couldn't. My internal frustration was mounting. It was all I could do to stop myself from shouting out, "Yes, but you're doing this all wrong."

It took more than a few rounds and a few story starters before I realized what I needed to learn. This was not my story. This was our story. I was trying to control the outcome instead of collaborating. I was thinking "Yes, but" instead of "Yes, and." I had to let go of my preconceptions and trust that as a team we would write the story that needed to be told.

That is much easier said than done, but when you keep that in mind and learn to trust the process not only will you and your team create a more effective pitch, you'll also enjoy the experience more.

> **PRO TIP:** "The connection you make through eye contact has a rhythm, a rhyme, and a reason. You are going to find that the We >Me concept of building your pitch starts with eye contact."
>
> —Rebecca Stuard, Executive Director, Improvolution.

Have Fun, No Matter What

Growing up in Queens often meant Saturday picnics on Long Island during the Summer. My parents loved the outings as much as my brother and me. My father would pack up the station wagon with a portable grill, charcoal briquettes, lawn chairs, blankets, and a cooler full of hot dogs, hamburgers, Coca Colas for us and Rheingold Beer for him and Mom. Then we would drive out on the Southern State Parkway to Sunken Meadow State Park.

One Saturday we woke up to rain. My parents waited a bit, hoping for clearing skies before deciding to cancel the picnic my brother and I had been looking forward to all week. Seeing the disappointment on our faces, my father came up with a Plan B.

He spread out our picnic blanket on the floor in the living room. He opened the door to the garage behind our second-floor apartment, set up the grill and barbequed while holding an umbrella over his head smiling and laughing the whole time. My father demonstrated how to have fun, no matter what curve balls might be placed in front of us. It was a lesson in real-time agility I have never forgotten.

There is always a way to turn things around—even when it seems insurmountable—and get through the bumpy spots with a bit of innovation, joy, and laughter. The trick, as my father taught me, is to learn to think on your feet.

There are things you can anticipate and troubleshoot and others you have to deal with in the moment. You can store your deck in the cloud and pray the room you are in has a stable WIFI, or you can keep a backup on a thumb drive.

Right before dress rehearsal for one of my NYU classes, I tested positive for COVID. I had three guest judges who had never met each other scheduled and 16 students showing up for something I organized. It was a big night, one I wanted to attend in-person but couldn't—at least not physically. After several emails, the help of my colleagues, a student willing to be my on-site point person, Zoom, and a lot of asking for help on my part, we pulled the evening off. It was not ideal, but it worked.

PRO TIP: Stuff happens that is out of your control. Learn to navigate it. Learn to laugh through it.

It's All About the Pitch

One of the dirty little secrets about the business world is that the best ideas do not always win. A beautifully designed presentation with a smart story arc and a great idea do not guarantee you anything if it is not presented well.

The pitch that wins the day is the one that is presented the best. The ones that win are presented the most convincingly. Winning pitches show, they don't tell. They persuade. They never lose sight of the problem that needs to be solved and how one specific idea accomplishes that. Some days that's easier to do than others.

Life gets in the way. We might be so concerned about closing the deal, getting the job, or convincing our boss our idea is the best thing since sliced bread was invented that our enthusiasm takes a backseat to worry. And there is nothing persuasive about worry.

Sometimes we get so caught up in talking that we forget to listen, not just with our ears but with our eyes. Body language can tell us a lot about an individual's reaction to our pitch or whether they are actively paying attention. If we are not listening with both our ears and our eyes, we cannot adapt in real time to keep our pitch moving in the direction we want it to go.

I have no idea how many pitches I have delivered in my career. Hundreds if not thousands. I've won a lot and lost a lot. The one thing that has been consistent in every single one is that moment of anxiousness before I am about to start.

Pitching your ideas can be a scary thing.

Imposter syndrome can set in. It happens to us all. Trust me, it has happened to me while writing this book. I have found myself questioning who I thought I was, to think I could write a book about pitching.

But I didn't stop. I kept going. My experience has shown me that a little anxiousness is not a bad thing. It's a good thing. If I wasn't the least bit anxious, something was wrong. A little anxiety means I care. It means I want to be my very best. The trick is to recognize the discomfort, turn that energy around, and use it to your advantage instead of letting it hold you back.

PRO TIP: "The one thing to remember when pitching is to always take a step back and think about the value you bring."

—Liz Kaplow, Founder and CEO, Kaplow Communications

Be Present

For many years I traveled West each winter to ski. There is something quite spectacular about standing at the top of a snow-covered mountain in the Colorado Rockies on a sun filled day with a blue sky as your backdrop.

As you point your skis downhill, the only thing you are thinking about is getting to the bottom. You are not thinking about the electric bill you forgot to pay or the fight you had with your significant other that morning. You are fully, 100 percent present.

You know you can't get from where you are to the bottom without first navigating each turn as you approach it. You literally cannot get ahead of your skis. You have to stay with them, looking no further than where you are in that moment.

You are present.

That is what you want to create for yourself when standing in front of a room about to begin your pitch.

Start by taking a moment to breathe.

Breathing sounds so much simpler than it is. When we get nervous, the wires in our brains get crossed, and we get stuck up in our heads. When we're in our heads, we forget to breathe. As soon as we do that, we are out of our bodies, and when that happens, we lose confidence.

Before you begin your presentation, take a deep breath, and give yourself a moment.

TRY THIS: When I am working on a project —like this book—I need to be fully present, with no distraction. The first thing I do is turn the Do Not Disturb function on my iPhone, which is synced with all my devices, so I have no message or email alerts to divert my attention. Next, I set my timer for the amount of time I want to work on the project. It keeps me present and fully focused and in the moment. Try it and see what happens!

Bring Passion to Your Pitch

When I started selling country music radio advertising, I did not have much passion for the product. It was not my favorite music genre, and I couldn't really understand how it would appeal to anyone else. But I needed the job, and I needed the money. I had to figure out how to find enthusiasm for what I was selling if I was going to succeed, I went about convincing myself of the radio station's value to the businesses and agencies I was pitching. Just because I didn't like it, didn't mean there was not a market for it.

I did my homework by conducting some research. I read articles, learned about the core listener and how engaged they were in the format. Going to live station events helped me realize the appeal. Data was not as easy as a keystroke away in the '80s, but I managed to find enough hard and grassroots data to convince myself of the value of the product and the audience it drew. That translated into enthusiasm when I was pitching my radio station.

That passion eventually turned into a lot of closed deals, revenue for the station, and big commission checks for me. As an added bonus: I gained an appreciation for that genre of music.

Sometimes it is easy to bring passion to your pitch. Other times you will have to work harder to find it. But you have to discover it.

You won't always get to work with the products and services you use or love the best, but that does not mean they have no value.

> **PITCH POINTER:** If you and your team are not passionate about your ideas, you are not going to convince anyone else to be.

Practice. Practice. Practice.

No matter how many times she has played, no matter how many Grand Slams she has won, Serena William continues to practice her game. She still practices, and she is no longer playing competitively.

Pitching with your team requires a similar kind of discipline. Practice helps you hone and refine the story you are telling. It may uncover things you might have missed, including something as seemingly insignificant as a typo on a slide or a selling point you need to emphasize more. Practice also allows you to time the length of your pitch and make sure you are keeping within a 20-minute maximum time. The more you rehearse, the more you can rely on muscle memory and not the slide deck.

When you practice alone, record yourself. Then play it back and listen. Are you using enough inflection in your voice? Talking too fast? Speaking with enough enthusiasm and persuasiveness? If you are boring yourself, ask yourself why and what you need to do to change that. Practice really does make perfect.

PRO TIP: "Spontaneity is the product of preparation."
—Peter Coughter, Author, The Art of the Pitch

Your Secret Weapon

I once had a student who sought out my advice as she prepared for an interview with L'Oreal. After it was over, I asked her how it went. She told me at the beginning she got very nervous, then she remembered something I had told her.

Take a breath and don't forget to be yourself.

We live in a time when too many of us are trying to be something or somebody we are not. Everyone is looking for the hidden formula that will get them the business or the job. In fact, all that's needed are some commonsense principles. Whether you are pitching a job or a business idea, do your homework, create a convincing story, practice, and be human.

That last element is critical: just be you.

P.S. She got the job!

PRO TIP: "Be yourself. The world worships the original."

—Ingrid Bergman

Be Your Best

When my mother died, the white letter-sized envelope that held a copy of her will contained a surprise. Inside was a second one that was labeled, "To be opened upon my demise."

Death was not a word that she and I used when we talked about the inevitable. When you are gone. When you join your friends on the other side. At your funeral. But never did either of us use the word death. I'm not sure why my mother settled on demise, but I suppose it sounds less triggering than death.

Inside that second envelope I found two smaller ones. One was for me and the other for my brother, Peter. Each was written in Mom's familiar script, finished with a flourish under each of our names— something she always did on the outside of an envelope.

I didn't know what to expect but I was sure she would not have written much, just enough to leave us each with some thought, a few last words when neither of us could talk back to her. While my mother had a knack for finding the perfect Hallmark card to express exactly what she wanted to say, she was not one to do so when penning her own words.

Her last note was brief, just enough to fill a small sheet of lined notepaper embossed with a bird and flowers in the top right corner, and (as I learned and should have expected) what she wrote me was identical to what she wrote to my brother. Having been the middle child of seven in a Greek-American family with only one sister, my mother made it a point to not favor one of us over the other.

She assured us both we had made her happy and proud over time and she wished us health and happiness in the years ahead. She reminded us to look out for each other and warned us that she would be watching over us, just in case we forgot. There is one line she wrote that has stuck with me and I carry with me every day.

"Always be the best you can be."

For as long as I can remember, I heard a version of that advice from her. Whether it was before a job interview or a party where I might meet new people, right before *"Be Careful"* came *"Be Your Best."* While I am sure there were times my mother encouraged me to "be the best," what I still hear her whisper in my ear every day is "be your best."

Be your best or be the best.

It's a choice we make. One keeps you in the moment and the other can take you out of it. A desire to be the best can defy the laws of the universe. It can force us to push too hard towards a desired goal and forget about the process. When we become fixated on the result, we get trapped in our heads instead of in our bodies, and this takes us out of the moment. And being in the moment is where we have all our power.

Being your best does not preclude doing the work and putting forth the effort. There is commitment to yourself to be your best that involves a lot of preparation and discipline. In fact, being your best is the only way to be the best.

Not everyone finishes in first place. It's a great feeling when we do, but the reality is not everyone is *the* best at everything, every day. Even when we are really good at what we do, we can still finish second.

When I teach my Real-World classes at NYU and the student teams get ready to compete for the final pitch, everyone wants to win. I get it. I want them all to win too, but that is not how life works. My mother understood that and made being your best her philosophy—and mine as well.

The purpose of this book has been to guide you through the process of creating and presenting a pitch that engages and sells. If you have done the work the only thing left to do on the day of your presentation is to give it your all and leave it on the floor. Have fun no matter what and enjoy the process. In the words of my mother, at that point all you can do is to be your best. The rest is out of your control.

ACKNOWLEDGEMENTS

When I first began teaching at NYU's School of Professional Studies, I was told that when you teach, you learn. This book, which would not exist if not for my graduate students, is a testament to that statement. In my Real-World Strategic Partnership classes, I learned that there was a need to simplify what it means to use story when crafting a pitch.

I am forever grateful to each and every one of the students who helped me to refine this framework with each iteration of their own pitches. To those students who read drafts of this when it was a work in progress, your "tough love" and thoughtful suggestions are evident in each page. Witnessing your success in delivering your "final pitches to the client" is what assured me that this framework has value.

Thanks to the many colleagues and friends I am so fortunate to know and who so willingly shared their wisdom for the pro tips. A special shout out to Dave Hollander who was the one who sought me out to teach my first Real-World class in 2018. There would be no framework without you.

Lastly, as always to my parents, Nancy and Jim. While you no longer walk this earth in a physical form, I hear your voices whispering in my ear and encouraging me every day. Your impact is evident in every word I write and every step I take. Love you both, always.

ABOUT THE AUTHOR

Joanne Tombrakos has been calling herself a storyteller since before it was the trendy thing to do. She has delivered thousands of pitches in every industry sector over the course of a successful twenty-five-year career that has included working at CBS, Time Warner Cable and NY1 News as a media sales and marketing executive. She prides herself that she never sold anybody anything, but she did learn to tell a very convincing story that closed a lot of business.

A marketing and business strategist recognized as an expert in personal branding, she uses those same skills today as an Assistant Professor of Marketing at NYU's School of Professional Studies and as the author of The Secrets They Kept, It Takes An Egg Timer: A Guide to Creating the Time for Your Life, and the workbook Getting Your Personal Brand Story Straight. She sits on the advisory board of the Paresa Collection and is the host of the podcast, Marketing, Mindfulness and Martinis.

While she currently resides on the other side of the Hudson River she is and always will consider herself a New Yorker. You can follow @joannetombrakos on most social networks or visit her website, joannetombrakos.com.

Made in the USA
Middletown, DE
18 February 2024

49987135R00078